Nature's Wonders

MOUNT EVEREST

Ann Heinrichs

Marshall Cavendish
Benchmark
New York

Marshall Cavendish Benchmark
99 White Plains Road
Tarrytown, NY 10591
www.marshallcavendish.us

Expert Reader: Tom Holzel, Mount Everest historian, former member of the American Alpine Club, Fellow 2005 at the Explorers Club, and published author of mountaineering articles

Library of Congress Cataloging-in-Publication Data
Heinrichs, Ann.
Mount Everest / by Ann Heinrichs.
p. cm. — (Nature's wonders)
Summary: "Provides comprehensive information on the geography, history, wildlife, peoples, and environmental issues of Mount Everest"—Provided by the publisher.
Includes bibliographical references and index.
ISBN 978-0-7614-3933-2
1. Everest, Mount (China and Nepal)—Juvenile literature. I. Title.
DS495.8.E9H45 2009
954.96—dc22
2008030050

Editor: Christine Florie
Publisher: Michelle Bisson
Art Director: Anahid Hamparian
Series Designer: Kay Petronio

Photo research by Connie Gardner

Cover photo by Ferdinando Tacconi, Hillary and Tensing
reach the summit of Mount Everest/The *Bridgeman Art Library*

The photographs in this book are used by permission and through the courtesy of:
Alamy: Galen Rowell/Mountain Light, 4; Peter Giovannini, 23; Arco Images, 36; David Woodfall, 79; *Peter Arnold*: Lynn and Donna Rogers, 33; *Art Life Images*: age footstock, 42; TMC Images, 63; *Getty Images*: Doug Allen, 8; Alex Cao, 14; Jake Norton, 16; Roger Mear, 19; Bobby Model, 22; Hulton Archive, 42; Stringer, 48; Paula Bronstein, 73; Barry Bishop, 74; Travel Ink, 85; Alan Kearney, 88; Mindn Pictures: Colin Monteath, 8, 31(B); Grant Dixon, 29(B); *SuperStock*: William Hamilton, 34; age footstock, 89; *AP Photo*: STR, 49, 81; *The Granger Collection*: 53; *Danita Delimont*: 10; Jon Arnold, 30(T); John Warburton Lee, 68–69; *Photo Researchers*: Andrew Clarke, 77; Corbis: David Keaton, 17; Craig Lovell, 26; Galen Rowell, 28, 37; Tiziana and Gianni Baldizzone, 29(T); John van Hasselt, 45, 64; Robert HoLmes, 56; Rob Howard, 58, 60; *Bridgeman Art Library*: Ferdinando Tacconi, Hillary and Tensing hack their way a step at a time along a ridge, 38; Royal Geographical Society, London, Sherwill W., Indian survey porters carrying equipment needed for task of mapping India, 40; Ferdinando Tacconi, Hillary and Tensing reach the summit of Mount Everest, 52; *The Image Works*, 47.

Maps (p. 6 and p. 15) by Mapping Specialists Limited

Printed in Malaysia

135642

CONTENTS

ONE

The Top of the World

This glistening peak, often shrouded in clouds, inspires an awe-struck reverence. Tibetan people call it *Chomolungma*, meaning Goddess Mother of the World. In the Nepali language, it is *Sagarmatha*, or Goddess of the Sky. Westerners call it Mount Everest. Regardless of its name, this jumble of rock, ice, and snow is the highest mountain on Earth. Its summit is literally the top of the world.

Mount Everest is a peak in Asia's great Himalaya Mountain range. In the ancient Sanskrit language of India, *Himalaya* means "the abode of snow." This snow-covered mountain system separates southern Asia from the Tibetan Plateau to the north. Nine of the world's ten highest peaks rise in the Himalayas. Towering over them all is the jagged, icy summit of Mount Everest. It straddles the border between Nepal and Tibet, more formally known as the Tibet Autonomous Region of China.

◄ *A mountaineer climbs the icy Rongbuk glacier on Mount Everest's north face.*

GEOPOLITICAL MAP OF MOUNT EVEREST

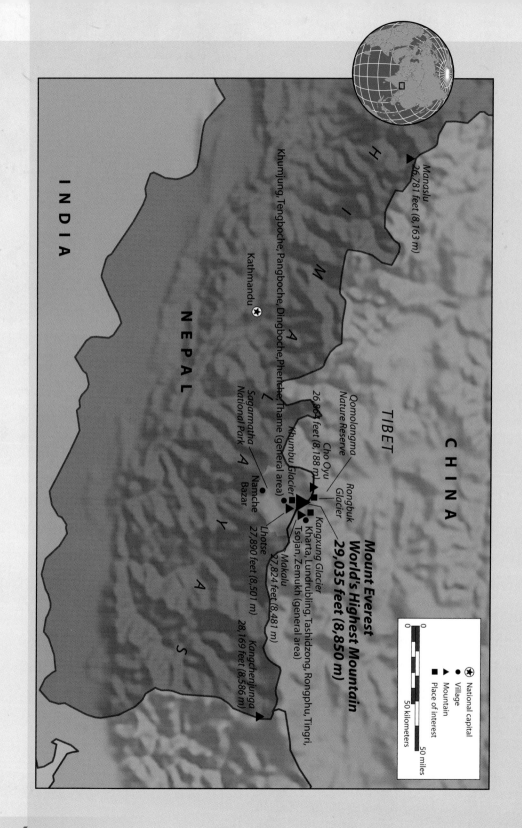

Manaslu
26,781 feet (8,163 m)

INDIA

NEPAL

H
I
M
A
L
A
Y
A
S

Kathmandu

Khumjung, Tengboche, Pangboche, Dingboche, Pheriche, Thame (general area)

TIBET

CHINA

Qomolangma
Nature Reserve

Cho Oyu
26,863 feet (8,188 m)

Rongbuk
Glacier

Khumbu Glacier

Sagarmatha
National Park

Namche
Bazar

Lhotse
27,890 feet (8,501 m)

Kangxung Glacier

Kharta, Lundrubling, Tashidzong, Rongphu, Tingri,
Tsojan, Zemukh (general area)

Makalu
27,824 feet (8,481 m)

Mount Everest
World's Highest Mountain
29,035 feet (8,850 m)

Kangchenjunga
28,169 feet (8,586 m)

⊛ National capital
● Village
▲ Mountain
■ Place of interest

0
50 kilometers

0
50 miles

The World's Ten Highest Peaks

MOUNTAIN	LOCATION	HEIGHT
Mount Everest	Nepal/Tibet	29,035 feet (8,850 m)
K2	Pakistan/China	28,250 feet (8,611 m)
Kanchenjunga	Nepal/India	28,169 feet (8,586 m)
Lhotse	Nepal/Tibet	27,940 feet (8,516 m)
Makalu	Nepal/Tibet	27,762 feet (8,462 m)
Cho Oyu	Nepal/Tibet	26,906 feet (8,201 m)
Dhaulagiri	Nepal	26,795 feet (8,167 m)
Manaslu	Nepal	26,781 feet (8,163 m)
Nanga Parbat	Pakistan	26,660 feet (8,126 m)
Annapurna	Nepal	26,545 feet (8,091 m)

Note: All are in the Himalayas except K2, which is in the Karakoram range.

THE CLIMBING FRENZY

For thousands of years Mount Everest remained just one of many peaks among the high Himalayas. Only in 1852 did geographers realize it was the world's highest mountain. Not content to simply gaze at this natural wonder, **mountaineers** were driven to climb it. Reaching the summit became their goal. That goal was reached in 1953 when New Zealand beekeeper Edmund Hillary and Nepalese Sherpa Tenzing Norgay stood on the top of the world.

Today, climbing Mount Everest remains the ultimate challenge for mountaineers. Thousands of people have joined the scramble to reach the top. Unfortunately, good sportsmanship has given way to careless climbing, self-centered ambition, and foolish decision making. More than 180 people have died in the quest for the summit. Yet, for those who succeed and live to relish their victory, it is their crowning achievement.

Many adventurous mountaineers pitch their tents in the deep snow of Mount Everest.

A Unique Environment

Mount Everest's landscape features rugged terrain, dramatic glaciers, and deep valleys. Many rare animal species make their homes there. So do thousands of Tibetan peoples such as the **Sherpas**, with their unique culture. Nepal established Sagarmatha National Park to protect this exceptional area. In addition, the United Nations Educational, Scientific and Cultural Organization (UNESCO) listed the park as a World Heritage site. This proclaims the Everest region as a site of worldwide importance.

Mount Everest's environment varies from lofty peaks to rugged slopes to green valleys. Here, yaks graze on a grassy hillside east of Mount Everest.

Environmentally speaking, all is not well at the top of the world. Decades of adventurers, drawn to the awesome peak, have left a shameful legacy. They have stripped firewood from the mountainsides and scattered trash on the slopes. The culture of the Sherpa people has been affected, too. Many have switched their livelihoods from farming and herding to mountaineering services. Fortunately, local people have organized programs to reclaim their natural resources. Environmentalist groups around the world are targeting the region, too. They hope to preserve Mount Everest's natural and cultural wonders for generations to come.

TWO

A Geographical Wonder

Yawning ravines, sheer rock walls, deep powdery snow, and tumbling blocks of ice—these are some of Mount Everest's features. High on the mountain, climbers face howling snowstorms, gale-force winds, thundering **avalanches**, and air so thin a person can hardly breathe. For many, the rough terrain and the dangers only add to the allure of the world's highest peak.

MEASURING THE MOUNTAIN

Just how high is Mount Everest? Teams of geographers have tried to settle this question for more than 150 years. Most have measured the mountain from a distance, using sophisticated **surveying** instruments. In 1954 surveyors from India measured the peak at 29,028 feet (8,848 meters) above sea level. This figure was an average of data taken from a dozen stations, each located miles from the peak. Like other measurements, though, it could easily have been different. Everest's rocky mountaintop is covered with ice and snow, which melts and builds up as the weather changes.

◀ *The topographical features of Mount Everest are some of the most dramatic in the world.*

The National Geographic Society sponsored a surveying expedition in 1999. This international team installed a global positioning system (GPS) unit in the highest point of rock beneath the ice and snow. Using other satellite-based data, they arrived at a figure of 29,035 feet (8,850 m). This is now widely recognized as the height of Mount Everest. Nepal and China, however, officially accept the earlier figure. Either way, the mountain is almost 5.5 miles (8.8 kilometers) high.

A Giant among Giants

Mount Everest rises amid a cluster of high Himalayan peaks. Makalu to the southeast and Cho Oyu to the northwest are the world's fifth and sixth highest mountains. Farther east is Kanchenjunga, the third highest. Just south of Everest is Lhotse, the world's fourth highest peak. Its base is actually connected to Mount Everest. To the southwest, Nuptse towers high above the landscape. It is considered part of the surrounding mountains rather than an independent peak. Changtse rises to the north of Everest, in Tibet. It is the world's forty-fifth highest mountain.

MILLIONS OF YEARS OF UPLIFT

Mount Everest's ascent to the top of the world took millions of years. It began with two tectonic plates, or giant masses of land. One was the Eurasian Plate, where Europe and Asia are now. The other was an island continent called the Indian Plate. It carried what is now the Indian subcontinent—India, Nepal, Pakistan, Bhutan, Bangladesh, Sri Lanka, and the Maldives. The Indian Plate drifted northward until, about 50 million years ago, it crashed into the Eurasian Plate. Seawater rushing between the two plates created the ancient Tethys Sea.

As the Indian Plate continued to push northward, it slipped beneath the Eurasian Plate. This forced the edge of the Eurasian Plate to buckle and rise upward. Over millions of years this meeting of plates pushed up the Himalaya Mountains. In the process, the Tethys Sea closed up. Its crumpled seabed was thrust up high among the rising peaks. This left a yellowish strip of limestone through the mountains full of fossilized sea creatures. On Everest and nearby peaks, this diagonal strip occurs at about 25,000 to 27,500 feet (7,620 to 8,400 m). Geologists and climbers call it the Yellow Band.

The Tibetan Plateau, just north of the Himalayas, also rose up. Today, this vast plain has an average height of about 14,800 feet (4,500 m). That is higher than most of the world's mountains.

Even now, the Indian Plate continues to push against Eurasia. As a result, the world's highest mountain is rising higher all the time. It grows a few millimeters every year. Mount Everest is gradually

The Tibetan Plateau is the highest and largest plateau on Earth.

shifting northeastward, too, moving about 2.4 inches (6 centimeters) a year.

THE SHAPE OF EVEREST

The top of Mount Everest is shaped like a pyramid with three sides, or faces. The border between Nepal and Tibet passes right through the summit. The North Face and the East Face, or Kangshung Face, are in Tibet. Only the Southwest Face is in Nepal.

Where Mount Everest's faces meet, they form ridges on the southeast, northeast, and west sides of the peak. Few climbers take a route directly up one of the faces. Instead, they climb up to one of the ridges, where they can get a better foothold.

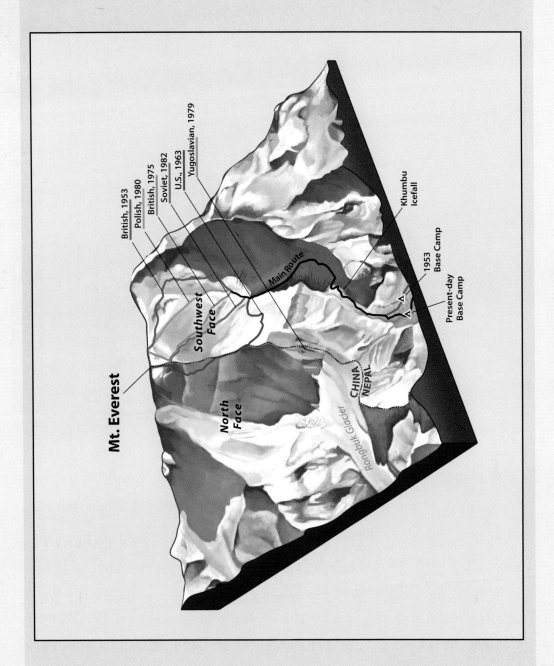

Mt. Everest

British, 1953
Polish, 1980
British, 1975
Soviet, 1982
U.S., 1963
Yugoslavian, 1979

Southwest Face

North Face

Main Route

Rongbuk Glacier

CHINA
NEPAL

Khumbu Icefall

1953 Base Camp

Present-day Base Camp

Climbers make their way up the South Summit of Everest. It is 28,704 feet high.

The southeast ridge, or southern route, from Nepal, is the most frequently climbed route. Along this ridge, not far from the summit, is a dome of ice and snow called the South Summit. Above that, the ridge narrows to what climbers call a knife-edge ridge. If they lose their footing here, they could plummet thousands of feet to their death. Next comes the Hillary Step, named for Edmund Hillary, who first reached the summit in 1953. This is a sheer rock face, 40 feet (12 m) high.

The northeast ridge, or northern route, in Tibet, is the second most popular route. As climbers approach the summit, they must scale three "steps," or steep rock faces. From here, they climb the steep snowfields of the summit pyramid.

Finally, at the top, is the coveted summit itself. This platform of hard-packed snow and ice—with a spectacular view from the top of the world—is said to be about the size of a picnic table.

The height of Mount Everest's summit is 29,035 feet. Here, climbers take in the view from the top of the world.

GLACIERS

Massive glaciers, or rivers of ice, cling to the slopes of the Himalayas. The glaciers flow like rivers, though much more slowly. Only Antarctica and Greenland store more freshwater than the Himalayan glaciers. They are the source of Asia's largest rivers, providing water to 1.3 billion people in India, Nepal, China, and Bhutan.

Rongbuk Glacier is the major glacier on Mount Everest's north side. Like many rivers, it is fed by so-called tributary glaciers—West Rongbuk Glacier and East Rongbuk Glacier. The central Rongbuk Glacier flows northward into the Rongbuk Valley. Among the tiny settlements in the Rongbuk Valley is Rongbuk Monastery. It is a center for Tibetan Buddhists in the region. Nearby is the Base Camp where climbers start their ascent of Mount Everest from the north side.

To reach Mount Everest's north side Base Camp, climbers must trek across Rongbuk Glacier.

Rongbuk Glacier's meltwater feeds the Rongbuk River. This river once provided abundant irrigation water for local farmers' barley crops, but the flow is much lighter today. Scientists believe this is because Rongbuk Glacier is retreating, or becoming smaller, due to global warming.

Glossary of Mount Everest's Features

col	(Welsh for "saddle") a mountain pass; a low ridge between two peaks
couloir	a steep-sided gorge or gully in a mountainside
crevasse	a large crack in a glacier, with vertical walls of ice
cwm	(pronounced *KOOM*; Welsh for "valley") a broad, flat, bowl-shaped valley of ice at the head of a glacier
icefall	a jumble of huge ice blocks that have tumbled down at the advancing edge of a glacier; dangerous because the ice blocks can be unstable and fall
ridge	the line where two mountain faces meet
serac	a tall peak of ice on a glacier, often forming where crevasses intersect; dangerous because it can suddenly collapse on climbers
snow bridge	snow that covers the opening of a crevasse; dangerous because a climber may fall through the snow into the crevasse

Kangshung Glacier, on the east side of Everest, feeds the Kama River. Both the Kama and the Rongbuk rivers eventually join the Arun River, which flows through a mountain pass into Nepal.

Khumbu Glacier is the major glacier on the Nepal side of Mount Everest. It skids down the mountainside at the rate of about 4 feet (1.2 m) a day. Meltwater from the Khumbu Glacier flows into Nepal's Dudh Kosi River. The Dudh Kosi River valley is the main route for travelers on Mount Everest's south side. Along the way, they pass many villages of Nepal's Sherpa people. North of the village of Pheriche is the base of Khumbu Glacier. High on the glacier is the Base Camp where climbers begin their ascent on this side of Everest.

CREVASSES, CWMS, AND COLS

As Khumbu Glacier heaves along, gaping cracks called crevasses open up, and enormous, house-sized slabs of ice break off and tumble down. This chaotic area, like a frozen river plunging over a cliff, is called the Khumbu Icefall. For Everest climbers, it is a major danger on their ascent.

Above the Khumbu Icefall is the Western Cwm. This is a broad, bowl-shaped valley scooped out by Khumbu Glacier. It looks like a round stadium surrounded by the peaks of Lhotse, Nuptse, and Everest. Deep crevasses crisscross the Western Cwm, some of them as wide as 80 feet (24 m). Snowfall forms snow bridges across the crevasses. Often just thin crusts of snow, these bridges can create

Mount Everest's climbers tackle Khumbu Icefall's ice towers and crevasses. It is the most dangerous part of the climb.

the illusion of solid ground, becoming a dangerous hazard for climbers. Oddly, the Western Cwm can be scorchingly hot because sunlight reflects on climbers from all sides. If the skies are clear and the wind is still, temperatures can reach 100 degrees Fahrenheit (38 degrees Celsius) or more. Climbers must wear dark sunglasses to protect their eyes, and sunburn is a serious concern.

Amid the jagged landscape of the Everest region are high mountain passes called cols. They are shaped like saddles, providing level routes between high peaks. On the Tibet side of Mount Everest, the North Col, at 23,000 feet (7,000 m), links Everest and Changtse. On the Nepal side, the South Col, at 26,000 feet (7,925 m), stretches

Ladders are used to cross a crevasse in the Western Cwm.

between Mount Everest and Lhotse. Lying at a much higher elevation than the North Col, the South Col marks the beginning of what is called the Death Zone. The air here is so thin, or low in oxygen, that humans cannot survive for long. Climbers usually breathe with oxygen tanks from this point on.

Snowy, Icy, Windy, and Cold

Climate conditions on Mount Everest can be severe. Violent winds, blinding snowstorms, and frigid temperatures can be life threatening, sometimes sweeping in without warning. Mount Everest's height creates an extra wind hazard. Its peak is in the lower reaches of the jet stream, a high-speed air current in the earth's atmosphere. Winds can whip across the summit at speeds of more than 100 miles (160 km) an hour.

Seasons on Mount Everest are not evenly spaced throughout the year. They revolve around the **monsoon**, a season of heavy snowstorms. Monsoon season, or summer, lasts from June roughly through September. This is when Mount Everest receives the heaviest precipitation. On the lower foothills, the monsoon begins with rain in late May or June. Soon clouds shroud the mountain, and treacherous storms dump tons of snow on the slopes. Some snow becomes hard and frozen, while some forms a layer of deep powder. July is Mount Everest's "warmest" month, but the temperature on the summit never rises above freezing. The average July temperature there is −2° Fahrenheit (−19 °C).

Autumn is usually called the postmonsoon season. It may begin as early as September if the monsoon is over by then. Temperatures begin to drop and, by mid-October, winter winds begin to rise. The snow is deep now from the monsoon snowfall. In spite of these conditions, many climbers approach Mount Everest in the autumn. Snow skiers even take to the slopes, too, to take advantage of the heavy snow cover.

By November, winter has set in. Winter storms from December through March bring even more snow. Winds reach an all-time high, lashing the summit at more than 170 miles (274 km) an hour. Temperatures at this time become bitterly cold. Mount Everest's coldest month is January, when the summit averages −33° Fahrenheit (−36 °C). With the wind, though, temperatures feel much colder.

Spring, in April and May, is usually called the premonsoon season. This is when temperatures begin to warm up, making the winter snows melt quickly. Rivers swell with the glaciers' meltwater, and wildflowers bloom across the high mountain meadows. On Everest, though, the spring thaw presents the danger of avalanches and collapsing ice. Nevertheless, most people attempt to climb the mountain in April or May, before the monsoon begins again. The jet stream shifts northward at this time, making it less windy around the mountaintop. Still, unpredictable winds and the low level of oxygen near the summit make climbing dangerous any time of the year.

THREE

Wildlife on Mount Everest

Glaciers and snowfields do not seem like a good habitat for wild-life. Not all of Mount Everest is cold and icy, though. Wildlife on the mountainsides depends on the altitude. High on the mountain, frigid conditions make it hard for both plants and animals to survive. However, a rich variety of wildlife thrives at lower elevations. Shaggy mountain goats, brilliantly colored birds, frisky monkeys, and rare snow leopards inhabit the rocky, forested slopes. Based on the climate at different altitudes, Mount Everest has several vegetation zones. Animals need plants for food and shelter, as they vary with the altitude as well.

VEGETATION ZONES

The lower slopes of Mount Everest are forested, with cone-bearing trees such as junipers, silver firs, hemlocks, and blue pines. Mixed in with them are oak trees and bamboo. Flowering evergreen shrubs such as rhododendrons flourish here, too. Brilliant red and pink rhododendron blossoms burst out in the spring. The forested zone

extends up to the tree line—the highest point where full-sized trees can grow. On Everest's south face, this point is at about 13,100 feet (4,000 m) above sea level. Tree lines vary by region, depending on location, slope, and local climate conditions.

Above the tree line is the alpine shrub and meadows zone. It extends up to about 15,500 feet (4,700 m). Plants there are small and hardy enough to survive the harsh wind and cold. They include shrubs and dwarf plants, as well as high-altitude grasses and flowers.

Once the first monsoon rains begin, the high meadows are green with grasses and blooming with brightly colored wildflowers. Local herders use this area as a summer grazing ground for their yaks. Dense thickets of dwarf juniper, dwarf rhododendrons, and other shrubby plants grow in this zone, too. They provide cover for many wild animals. Dwarf junipers, also called shrub junipers, are commonly harvested for firewood.

◄ *Rhododendrons bloom in the Valley of Flowers, east of Mount Everest.*

The next level is the upper alpine zone. This is the highest level where plants can flourish. Only species such as lichens and mosses that can withstand extreme cold survive here. *Arenaria* species, called alpine cushion plants, also live in this zone. They grow in a tight, ground-hugging mound that looks like a cushion. They, too, are often gathered for fuel.

A herd of yaks graze on a high, open meadow.

Alpine cushion plants grow in the upper alpine zone.

The Arctic zone begins at about 18,000 feet (5,500 m) on Mount Everest's southern slope and 19,000 feet (5,800 m) on the northern slope. This permanent snow line is covered with snowfields, glaciers, and ice year round. Researchers have found a few plant species at this level. However, beyond 20,000 feet (6,100 m), no plants can survive.

The Yak:
An All-Purpose Animal

Yaks can thrive at more high altitudes than any other large mammal in the world. They have been known to climb as high as 20,000 feet (6,100 m) to graze. Their large lungs can absorb oxygen in thin air, and their thick, shaggy coats keep them warm. In Tibetan, the male is called a yak, and the female is called a *dri*.

Yaks transport equipment and supplies for Mount Everest climbing expeditions. Their broad hooves make them sure-footed climbers. Carrying loads of up to 220 pounds (100 kilograms), they trudge through deep snow and up the icy mountain passes. For farmers, the yak is a source of meat, milk, and wool. Its milk is made into butter and cheese, and its hair is woven to make clothes, blankets, ropes, and tents. Yak droppings are also burned as fuel. Yaks are known for being cranky and hard to control. They are sometimes crossbred with cattle to produce the *dzo* (female, *dzomo*), a much more manageable animal.

Mammals

Mount Everest's animals are uniquely adapted to their environment. For example, their lungs can process air containing lower levels of oxygen. Mammals here have thick coats to protect them from the wind and cold. Some hibernate, or go into a deep sleep, during the winter when food is scarce.

Wildlife on the Nepal side of Mount Everest is protected within Sagarmatha National Park. Many rare, threatened, and endangered species live there. One is the shaggy, brown Himalayan tahr. This wild goat can be seen scrambling up and down steep, rocky slopes. Its hooves have a rubbery core that allows them to grip smooth surfaces. Tahrs graze in the high meadows in the summer and migrate

Himalayan tahrs are most active early in the day, spending the afternoon hours resting among rocks and vegetation.

Sagarmatha National Park

Nepal has designated the southern slope of Mount Everest, all the way up to its peak, as Sagarmatha National Park. It lies within Nepal's Solu-Khumbu district, with a visitors' center near the village of Namche Bazar. The lower reaches of the park enclose forests and grazing land. Many rare animals are protected there, including musk deer, wild yaks, snow leopards, Himalayan black bears, and red pandas. Armed guards are stationed at several points in the park to ward off hunters.

to lower levels in the winter. Two similar creatures are the serow and its smaller relative the goral. Both are goatlike animals that graze on the high, rocky slopes.

Another rare species is the musk deer. It is hunted for its musk, a substance contained in the male's scent gland below the abdomen. The musk is used in perfumes, and it is falsely believed to be a strength-giving drug. That belief makes musk one of the most expensive substances in the world, selling for as much as $20,000 per pound (per 0.45 kg). Hunters can remove the musk from live deer, but most just kill the animal.

Snow leopards are endangered worldwide because they are hunted for their luxurious fur skins. By the 1960s they had disappeared from the Everest region. Thanks to aggressive protection efforts, snow leopards have made a comeback, though they are still rare. They prey on large animals such as tahrs and deer.

Himalayan black bears roam among Everest's forested lower slopes. They feed on grasses, wild fruits and berries, and sometimes small animals. These bears are mainly nocturnal, grazing at night and sleeping in rock crevices or thick undergrowth during the day. In the autumn, they eat extra food to fatten up for winter, when they

Though it thrives in extreme environments, the snow leopard's survival is in jeopardy due to poachers and loss of habitat.

hibernate. Like other large animals in the region, their numbers have been reduced because of hunting.

Red pandas, also known as lesser pandas, are another rare species in the Everest region. They look nothing like their larger cousins, the familiar black-and-white pandas. Instead, they are small and reddish brown, with a long, bushy tail with stripes around it. They live on the lower mountain slopes, where they mostly feed on the leaves and tender shoots of *malingo,* a type of bamboo. Red pandas are threatened both by hunting and by the disappearance of their forest habitat.

Red pandas grow to about the size of a house cat, though their tails add an additional 18 inches to their length.

Common langurs are long-tailed monkeys that range from silvery gray to golden brown. They eat leaves and fruits, traveling in groups in the trees or on the ground. Other mammals roaming the mountainsides are mountain foxes, golden jackals, weasels, martens, civets, moles, shrews, and Himalayan mouse hares, or pikas.

The Yeti—Fact or Fiction?

For centuries, Sherpa and Tibetan villagers have told tales of the yeti—a huge, hairy creature of the Mount Everest region that walks upright like a human. Englishmen named it the abominable snowman. A similar creature, bigfoot, is said to roam the forests of North America. Many people claim to have seen evidence of the yeti on the high mountain slopes. In 1974 a Sherpa girl who was grazing her yaks reported a yeti attack. Villagers later found several yaks with their necks broken. Even famous mountaineers have reported seeing dark, humanlike figures in the distance. Others have spotted large, humanlike footprints in the snow. Still, no clear proof of the yeti's existence has been discovered, and the mystery remains.

BIRDS

More than one hundred bird species live among the forests, shrubs, and high meadows of Mount Everest. One of the most beautiful species is the Impeyan pheasant, Nepal's national bird. Nepalis call it the *danphe*, and it is also known as the Himalayan monal. Adult males glisten with brilliant colors ranging from metallic green and blue to coppery red, with a feathered crest on their head. Females have dull coloring, with brownish black plumage. Impeyan pheasants are large birds, reaching a length of about 28 inches (71 cm).

Blood pheasants are another common species. They are named for the reddish feathers on the male's breast, throat, and forehead. Blood pheasants spend most of their time on the ground and do not fly much. On the other hand, choughs (pronounced *chuffs*) are known for their acrobatic flight. They glide and loop through the air, landing expertly on rocky cliffs, where they build their nests. Red-billed choughs and yellow-billed choughs are common birds in the Everest region. Members of the crow family, they have glossy black feathers.

The male Impeyan pheasant is known for its multi-colored plumage.

Snow pigeons travel in huge flocks, circling through the sky before landing in a meadow. Tibetan snowcocks blend in well with the snowy, rocky landscape. Their feathers are mottled white, gray, and brown. Their loud cackle gives them away, though. Snowcocks are very tame around humans and may even eat out of their hands.

Large birds of prey soar over the mountainsides hunting for small animals to eat. They include golden eagles, Himalayan griffons, and lammergeiers, also called bearded vultures. Brahminy ducks, crested grebes, pintails, and other waterbirds live in the Gokyo Lake region. This wetland is also a haven for birds passing through the Himalayas on their migrations. Because local people consider Gokyo Lake a holy lake, they are careful to protect its wildlife from harm.

The Himalayan griffon is a vulture seldom seen below 4,000 feet.

FOUR

The Quest to Conquer

For thousands of years, the world's highest mountain remained a little-known peak among the high Himalayas. Its summit could hardly be distinguished from surrounding peaks. That began to change in the 1800s when India was under Great Britain's control. British merchants, governors, scientists, and explorers took notice of this intriguing mountain. They set out to map it, to measure it, and eventually, to climb it.

TO MAP AND MEASURE

How did Great Britain get involved with Mount Everest, a peak thousands of miles from Britain? It began in 1600 when a group of British merchants formed the British East India Company. Its aim was to carry on trade with India and other Asian lands. The trading company became the virtual ruler of India, and eventually, India became a British colony. In 1767 the British East India Company organized the Survey of India. This venture would survey, measure, and map the territories under the company's control.

◄ *The desire to climb and conquer Mount Everest has been a goal of many mountaineers since the late 1800s.*

An even bigger surveying project began in the early 1800s—the Great Trigonometric Survey. Its mission was to map British territory in India and to measure the highest Himalayan peaks. Surveyors used a system called triangulation to calculate locations. Using massive telescopic instruments called theodolites and 100-foot (30-m) steel chains, they established distances and heights by measuring angles and sides of triangles. This resulted in a grid of triangles covering most of the country.

Beginning in southern India, the surveyors gradually moved northward. In 1834 they reached the border of Nepal in the foothills

Surveyors map and measure British territory in India on the orders of the British East India Company.

of the Himalayas. Nepal was closed to foreigners at the time, so they surveyed east and west along the border. From there, they took measurements of dozens of Himalayan peaks, naming them with Roman numerals. Everest was just called Peak XV.

Finally, after years of measuring and remeasuring, surveyors realized that Peak XV might be the highest of all the peaks. All that remained was to calculate its height. This job fell to an Indian mathematician named Radhanath Sikdar. In 1852, working with dozens of measurements taken from many locations, Sikdar calculated that Peak XV was 29,000 feet (8,839 m) high. This was much taller than any other peak in the world. Even with the instruments and methods of the mid-1800s, Sikdar came remarkably close to the figure we know today.

Sikdar's superiors felt a round number might look suspicious, so they announced the peak's height as 29,002 feet (8,840 m). Because Peak XV was not considered a suitable name for such a special peak, British officials renamed it Mount Everest. This was to honor Sir George Everest, who had been the British surveyor-general of India for many years. Everest himself opposed the name, saying that local people could neither spell nor pronounce it in their native language. Nevertheless, Britain's Royal Geographical Society adopted the name.

Mount Everest is named after George Everest, who served as surveyor general of India.

In the British spirit of sports competition, the next challenge was to climb the mountain.

WHAT IT TAKES TO CLIMB

Even today, Mount Everest is hard to reach and hard to climb. Mountaineers once had to travel long distances on foot with all their gear on pack animals just to get near the mountain. Over the years, some roads and airstrips have been built in the region. Still, modern climbers have only footpaths, then no paths, once the mountain is reached.

A Sherpa carries a heavy load across the slopes of the Himalayan Mountains.

Typically, climbers ascend Mount Everest in teams of two to a dozen or more. The full climbing support crew is much larger, though. Ever since the earliest climbs, Nepal's Sherpa people have served as porters, and more recently as guides. Hardy, high-altitude mountaineers, they easily scramble up the mountainsides with heavy loads on their backs. They carry tents, food, a stove, oxygen tanks, medical supplies, and climbing equipment.

Once on the mountain, climbers face many physical risks. These hazards are serious, and some can be deadly. First, there are the obvious dangers of

Medical Risks of Mountaineering

Besides the physical risks of climbing Mount Everest, there are many medical hazards. Acute mountain sickness (AMS) is one of the most life-threatening conditions on Everest climbs. It sets in when the body has not adjusted to a decrease in oxygen levels. The first symptom of AMS is usually a headache. Then comes an array of symptoms—weakness, dizziness, loss of appetite, nausea, vomiting, shortness of breath, chest pains, and mental confusion. People with AMS symptoms must be given oxygen and descend to a lower altitude or they will die.

Exposure to cold leads to frostbite, cutting off blood circulation to the fingers, toes, or nose. These body parts may have to be amputated. Cold can also cause hypothermia, a lowering of the body temperature until the person basically freezes to death. Bright sunlight reflecting off the snow and ice can cause snow blindness. This painful condition can lead to temporary or even permanent blindness. Humidity, or air moisture, can be very low at high altitudes. This irritates the lungs, causing what is called the Khumbu cough. A person can cough so hard that he or she breaks a rib.

Climbers can prevent most of these conditions by planning wisely, climbing sensibly, and bringing proper protective gear. Some climbers are tempted to hide injuries or illnesses in their desire for the summit. This endangers not only their own lives but their teammates' lives as well. Expert mountaineers know it is more heroic to preserve human life than to reach a climbing goal, but this sentiment is not always shared by ambitious amateurs.

plummeting down the mountainside, dropping into crevasses, getting buried in avalanches, and being crushed by falling rocks or ice. One of the most serious hazards, though, is lack of oxygen.

The higher a person climbs, the less oxygen there is in the air. At 16,400 feet (5,000 m), the air contains only about half the oxygen available at sea level. On the summit, the oxygen content is down to one-third. Climbers have to ascend slowly so their bodies can acclimatize, or get used to the ever-thinning air. For every 1,000 feet (300 m) of climbing, they need to rest at least a day. Another rule of thumb is "climb high, sleep low." That is, they climb up during the day and climb down to a lower elevation to sleep.

When climbers reach about 25,600 feet (7,800 m), they enter the so-called Death Zone. From here on up, the body can acclimate no further, and most climbers must use supplemental oxygen. Once in the Death Zone, people have a small window of opportunity for reaching the summit. They must climb up and get back down quickly before the oxygen shortage endangers their lives.

Climbers have staked out about eighteen different routes to Mount Everest's summit. They ascend the peak's ridges and even the sheer faces. Most of these trails are incredibly dangerous, though. There are really two main climbing routes—the northeast ridge from Tibet and the southeast ridge from Nepal. Early mountaineers approached Everest from Tibet.

At Everest Base Camp a climber checks oxygen supplies that will be used when they reach 25,600 feet.

EARLY ATTEMPTS

British adventurers began setting their sights on Mount Everest as early as the 1890s. They faced political obstacles on both the north and south sides of the mountain. On the south side, monarchs of the Rana regime were bent on isolating Nepal from the outside world. Tibet, on the north side, was closed to foreigners, too. At the time, Tibet was a Buddhist domain under the leadership of the thirteenth Dalai Lama. This revered spiritual leader was considered the **reincarnation** of a long line of Buddhist masters. Tibet did not welcome non-Buddhist visitors, especially those who would trespass on the sacred mountain. Finally, though, in 1920 British officials persuaded the Dalai Lama to grant them permission to explore Mount Everest.

No one knew what hazards lay ahead on Everest, or even whether a human could survive the climb. The sport of mountaineering had spread through Europe, and it was catching on in Great Britain, too. Early mountaineers targeted the Alps mountain range in Europe. Thus, *alpinism* came to mean the same as *mountaineering*. Dressed in gentlemanly tweed suits, and armed with sturdy walking sticks, mountaineers struggled with peaks half as high as Everest.

In 1921 Britain's Royal Geographical Society and Alpine Club organized the first Everest expedition. The nine-man team was to explore possible routes up the mountain, mapping and snapping photos along the way. After studying the mountain from many angles, they ascended as far as the North Col, at 23,000 feet (7,000 m).

One team member was Alexander Kellas, a doctor and scientist with a zest for mountaineering. A veteran Himalayan climber, he had also done many studies on the body's reaction to low oxygen levels at high altitudes. Kellas had concluded that "Mount Everest could be ascended by a man of excellent physical and mental constitution in first-rate training" without using an artificial oxygen source. Sadly, Kellas himself died of a heart attack on his way to join the expedition.

Another British expedition was launched in 1922. This time they reached 27,300 feet (8,320 m). Tragedy struck this attempt, too, as an avalanche on the North Col slopes swept seven Sherpa porters over a cliff to their death. Some climbers began to wonder if the mountain was not meant to be climbed after all.

The 1922 expedition set up camp on the Rongbuk Glacier.

BECAUSE IT'S THERE

George Mallory had been a member of both British expeditions. On speaking tours, he thrilled audiences with his Everest adventures, and he became a favorite among mountaineering fans. Over and over, journalists asked him the same obvious question: why climb Mount Everest? At one point, according to a *New York Times* reporter, the exasperated Mallory answered with the now-famous phrase, "Because it's there."

Next came the 1924 expedition. The twelve-man team included Mallory, several other experienced mountaineers, twenty-two-year-old novice climber Andrew Irvine, and photographer John Noel.

George Mallory was a British climber who participated in three Everest climbs. He died during his third attempt in 1924.

Noel organized fundraising and publicity campaigns, including special commemorative postcards to be sent back to schoolchildren from Base Camp.

High winds and heavy snow plagued the team all the way. Yet higher and higher they climbed, struggling in pairs across the snow and up the icy slopes. One member, Edward Norton, reached 28,100 feet (8,565 m) before exhaustion and snow blindness forced him back down. This was a record height for a mountain climber, unbroken until 1953. But it was two other climbers who made this expedition famous.

On the morning of June 6, Mallory and Irvine had a breakfast of fried sardines and set out from their campsite on the North Col. Already they had overcome many of Everest's toughest challenges. Based on earlier experiences, they had decided to use bottled oxygen from here on up. By June 8 the summit was within reach, and today, they felt, would be the day.

Mallory's climbing gear astounds modern climbers. His clothing seems more like casual sportswear than serious mountaineering gear. He wore a button-down silk shirt, a pinstriped flannel shirt, suspenders, a wool sweater, a tweed coat, long woolen underwear, a fur-lined leather flying helmet, two pairs of gloves, three pairs of socks, and hobnail boots. He carried an ice axe, and he wore snow goggles.

Mallory and Irvine were last seen climbing a sheer rock face a few hundred feet from the summit. Then, misty, swirling clouds hid them from view, and they were never seen again. They had simply vanished into thin air. What happened? How far did they climb? Did they reach the summit? These remain burning questions to this day.

British mountaineers George Mallory and Andrew Irvine prepare for their climb up Mount Everest. This is the last image of them before they disappeared.

An Unattainable Goal?

The mountaineering community, and the world, mourned the loss of Mallory and Irvine. Nevertheless, the quest for the summit continued. Official British teams tried again in 1933, 1935, 1936, and 1938.

A remarkably odd character, Maurice Wilson, tried the climb alone in 1934. An inexperienced climber, Wilson relied instead on faith. He was sure he could reach the top of Everest through prayer and spiritual power alone. A year later, his body was found wrapped in a tent at 21,000 feet (6,400 m). The last entry in his diary read, "Off again, gorgeous day."

Again, political conditions foiled attempts on Everest. World War II (1939–1945) put a halt to climbing for years. Then, in 1950, China invaded Tibet and took over the Buddhist state. The northern approach to Everest, familiar by now to experienced British mountaineers, was closed off. In 1951 British climbers got permission from Nepal to approach the mountain from the south. This team explored the route, discovered its hazards, and established likely campsites along the way. Two separate Swiss teams attempted the south route in 1952. As on the northern route, the summit remained beyond reach.

Hillary and Tenzing: "A Few More Whacks"

More than four hundred people gathered in Kathmandu, Nepal's capital, for the 1953 expedition. Only a dozen of them made up the official climbing team. They included team leader and veteran climber John Hunt and a New Zealand beekeeper named Edmund Hillary. Among the others were 20 Sherpa guides and 362 porters.

They set off in March, as winter was beginning to wane. With several tons of baggage, they trekked through 175 miles (282 km) of countryside to Namche Bazar. From there, the team did practice climbs and tested out their equipment. Nepal was granting only one Everest permit per year, and the next few years were already booked up. This was their only chance to reach the summit for a long time, so all had to go well.

By May, the team was high on the mountainside, tantalizingly close to the peak. One pair of climbers advanced within 328 feet (100 m) of the top, but their oxygen equipment failed to work properly. Then Hunt selected Hillary and Sherpa Tenzing Norgay to make the next attempt. This was Tenzing's seventh Everest climb and Hillary's second. They pitched their tent high on an icy ledge for the night. As fierce winds whipped around the tent, they feasted on sardines and canned apricots, dates, jam, and honey.

On May 29, after a few hours of sleep, they awoke to sunny skies and a temperature of −17° Fahrenheit (−27 °C)—not bad for this height. They gobbled down more sardines and crackers and crawled out of their tent at 6:30 AM, hoisted oxygen cylinders onto their backs, and set out for the summit. Five hours later, the two became the first people ever to stand atop Mount Everest. In Hillary's words, "A few more whacks of the ice axe in the firm snow, and we stood on top."

Edmund Hillary and Tenzing Norgay were the first to conquer Mount Everest.

Hillary and Tenzing planted four flags on the peak—those of Great Britain, Nepal, India, and the United Nations. Tenzing dug a hole in the snow and placed in it some chocolate, an offering to the Buddhist spirits. Nearby, Hillary placed a Christian cross Hunt had given him. Then the two descended, to be greeted by worldwide acclaim for their historic feat.

CLIMBING EVEREST: NO END IN SIGHT

Hillary and Tenzing had such a grueling time climbing Mount Everest that they figured no one else would ever try it. They were wrong. Now every ambitious mountaineer had to do it, too. Hundreds of climbers poured into the dusty streets of Namche Bazar, where they stocked up on supplies and marched up to Base Camp. Airstrips were built in the Khumbu Valley to accommodate all the incoming trekkers. Climbers became ever more high-tech, using fixed ropes, harnesses, aluminum ladders, and GPS systems. They learned to wear polar fleece insulation, GORE-TEX® outerwear, neoprene facemasks, and other protective clothing.

Sir Edmund Hillary

Edmund Hillary (1919–2008) was one of the greatest adventurers
of modern times. Born in Auckland, New Zealand, he began climbing mountains as a teenager. As an adult, he made his living as a
beekeeper and continued to climb, scaling many Himalayan peaks.
In 1953, Hillary (below left) and his Sherpa guide, Tenzing Norgay
(below right), became the first people to reach the top of Mount
Everest. In honor of his achievement, the queen of England dubbed

Hillary a knight. He went
on to explore Antarctica, the
North Pole, and other chal-
lenging locations. Hillary
devoted much of his life to
helping the Sherpa people.
In 1960 he established the
Himalayan Trust to build
schools, hospitals, and airstrips for them. Concerned
about the Everest region's
degrading environment, he
also persuaded the Nepalese
government to establish
Sagarmatha National Park.

The urge to set new records was strong. In 1978 Reinhold Messner and Peter Habeler became the first to reach the summit without an oxygen tank. Others competed to be the youngest, oldest, or fastest climber, the first to take a certain route, the first from their country, and so on.

Landmark Everest Events

YEAR	CLIMBER	NATIONALITY	ACHIEVEMENT
1953	Edmund Hillary, Tenzing Norgay	New Zealander, Nepalese	First to reach the summit
1960	Wang Fu-chou, Chu Ying-hua, Konbu	Tibetan	First to reach the summit on the Tibet side
1963	James Whittaker	American	First American to reach the summit
1975	Junko Tabei	Japanese	First woman to reach the summit
1978	Reinhold Messner, Peter Habeler	Italian, Austrian	First summit without supplemental oxygen
1980	Reinhold Messner	Italian	First solo summit (also without supplemental oxygen)
2000	Davo Karnicar	Slovenian	First descent from the summit on skis
2003	Ming Kipa Sherpa	Nepalese	Youngest person to reach the summit (female, age 15)
2004	Pemba Dorje Sherpa	Nepalese	Fastest ascent (8 hours, 10 minutes)
2008	Apa Sherpa	Nepalese	Most times to the summit (18)
2008	Min Bahadur Sherchan	Nepalese	Oldest person to reach the summit (age 76, 11 months)
May 22, 2008	—	various	Most people to reach the summit from the Nepal side in one day (at least 75)

Note: Records are accurate as of December 2008.

It was inevitable that tragic records would be set, too. On May 10–11, 1996, eight people died trying to climb Everest. In all, fifteen people died that year, making it Everest's deadliest year ever. That same year, Tenzing Norgay's son, Jamling Tenzing Norgay, reached the summit. He did it to honor his father, and it would be a one-time-only event: "I promised my wife that after Everest, I would never climb again."

People still remembered Mallory and Irvine, who had disappeared on the 1924 expedition. Seventy-five years later, in 1999, a team set out to find their bodies. They found Mallory, conducted a brief religious service for him, and buried his remains on the icy slopes where he had fallen. Andrew Irvine's body has not yet been found.

In 2002 preparations were underway for the fiftieth anniversary of the 1953 ascent by Hillary and Tenzing. The two men's sons took part with a commemorative climb. True to his promise, Jamling went only as far as Base Camp, while Peter Hillary went on to the top.

Political conditions affected Mount Everest again in 2008 when China hosted the Olympic Games. As a publicity event, China sponsored a multiethnic expedition of climbers who carried the Olympic torch to the top of Mount Everest. The climb took place amid worldwide protests against China's takeover of Tibet. To suppress protesters, China banned all other climbers from the peak while the Olympic Torch team was there.

LOSING PERSPECTIVE

By 2008 more than three thousand people had reached the summit. At the same time, about 80 percent of those who try for the top fail to reach it. Mount Everest, once the realm of professional climbers, is now available to anyone who pays the necessary fees. So many people swarm the slopes that they create traffic jams. Other climbers can be stuck waiting an hour or two behind them, losing valuable time and depleting their precious oxygen supplies. Ambition often wins out over ethics, too. In 2006 dozens of people marched past British climber David Sharp as he lay dying on the mountainside.

Today, many climbers attempt to climb Mount Everest, sometimes creating "traffic jams" on the mountain.

Inexperienced climbers, hungry for bragging rights, make bad decisions and foolish mistakes. These mistakes can be deadly. Even experienced climbers may fall or run out of oxygen. More than two hundred people have died while climbing Mount Everest. In fact, the Death Zone has been called a "field of corpses." The frozen bodies are too heavy to remove from the icy slopes. Yet, people will still try to conquer Mount Everest—"because it's there."

Over the years, Jamling Tenzing Norgay developed a certain wisdom about the mountain. "[W]hen you climb this mountain you have to climb . . . as if [you are] a child crawling up to its mother's lap," he said. "You don't conquer Mount Everest. We believe climbing with pride, arrogance and disrespect can lead to trouble . . . where people are climbing for the wrong reason and people are climbing who should not be there at all."

FIVE

People of Chomolungma

For people of the Everest region, the high Himalayas are the abodes of gods, goddesses, and good and evil spirits. Among them is Mount Everest, or Chomolungma—the Goddess Mother of the World. This glistening, glacier-topped peak is the home of a beloved spiritual protector.

Traditionally, local people did not climb Mount Everest. This was partly out of reverence and partly because they had nothing to gain by climbing it. They lived in its shadow for hundreds of years, farming and tending their herds. In time, Westerners introduced a new culture that valued competitive climbing. This gave people new ways to make a living. Nevertheless, their centuries-old culture remains very much alive.

SHERPA TRADITIONS

Because of its altitude and climate, the Mount Everest region is sparsely populated. One group of people who thrive there are the Sherpas of Nepal. Sherpas are a Tibetan ethnic group, and their

◄ *The Sherpa make their home in the Everest region.*

Sherpas harvest their barley crop.

language is related to modern Tibetan. They originated in the eastern Tibetan province of Kham. In the 1500s they migrated over the Nangpa La pass into Nepal's Khumbu Valley. Today, about 3,500 Sherpas live in Nepal's Solu-Khumbu region, where Mount Everest is.

Sherpas live higher than almost any other people on Earth, thriving at altitudes up to 14,000 feet (4,270 m). They have developed extraordinary physical adaptations to their mountainous environment. With short, muscular bodies, they carry loads of 100 pounds (45 kg) or more for miles up the steep mountain slopes. Their blood pressure is low, and their lungs and bloodstream have a high capacity for absorbing oxygen. Compared to non-Sherpas, their muscles work more efficiently and blood reaches their brain more quickly. Scientists still do not completely understand how and why Sherpas' bodies work so well.

Traditionally, Sherpas are farmers, herders, and traders. One of their main crops is barley, a grain that thrives at high altitudes. Potatoes were introduced from India in the 1850s, and they became a valuable, high-calorie food crop. Sherpa herders graze their yaks in the high mountain meadows during the spring and summer, then move the herds to lower ground in the winter. For centuries, Sherpas engaged in trade with Tibet, carrying goods by yak through the Nangpa La pass. This trade has dwindled since the 1950s, with the Chinese occupation of Tibet.

Most Sherpa settlements in the Everest region lie along the Dudh Kosi River valley. One is Namche Bazar, an important Sherpa market town in the region. Farther north on the mountainside are the villages of Khumjung, Tengboche, Pangboche, Dingboche, and Pheriche. Pangboche is the highest village where people live year-round. Above this point, winter climate conditions are too harsh for survival.

Sherpas' naming traditions can be confusing to Westerners. A newborn child may be given two names—one by its family and another by the local lama, or religious teacher. The given name may consist of one or two words. Sometimes a Sherpa may change his or her name, believing this will assure a better future. Some Sherpas use one of eighteen traditional clan names as their surname, while others use the name *Sherpa* as a surname. Adding to the confusion, the surname may appear before or after the given name. However, many Sherpas go by only one one-word name.

A Buddhist Way of Life

Sherpas practice the Buddhist faith. It is based on the teachings of Siddhartha Gautama, called the Buddha, who was born in India in the 500s BCE. Buddhism teaches compassion for all beings and relief from suffering through good thoughts and deeds. The great teacher Padmasambhava, also called Guru Rinpoche, brought Buddhism to the Tibet region in the 700s CE. In Tibetan Buddhism, the spiritual goal is to achieve enlightenment in order to help others.

Religion shapes many aspects of Sherpa life. Most homes have a small, candlelit shrine, and people begin their day with offerings and prayers. Throughout the Solu-Khumbu region, boulders called *mani* stones are painted or carved with prayers and sacred symbols. Stupas (also called chortens) stand in every village. These religious monuments contain the relics, or remains, of a holy person. Strings of prayer flags are draped from boulders and trees. Each flag is inscribed with a prayer, so that the prayer ascends to the skies with each flutter of the breeze.

Buddhist monasteries can be found on the lower slopes of Mount Everest. They are spiritual retreats where red-robed monks devote their time to prayer, meditation, and study. The abbot is the head monk in each monastery, and lamas are monks who teach religious principles and perform rituals. The most famous monasteries on the Nepal side are Tengboche, Pangboche, and Thame. On the Tibet side, Rongbuk Monastery is the major monastery. Sherpas and other

Colorful prayer flags are placed near Mount Everest by those who hope for spiritual protection on their climb.

local people support their monasteries and take part in religious festivals there throughout the year.

Tengboche Monastery stands along the main route to Everest Base Camp. Thousands of visitors come every year. Some continue on to Mount Everest, while others visit only to enjoy the peaceful surroundings and spectacular mountain views. Buddhism teaches peace and compassion, and killing any living creature is prohibited. Thus, the wild animals roaming around Tengboche are unafraid of humans and remarkably tame. Both Sherpas and other Everest climbers stop at the monastery for blessings upon their expedition.

Monastery Life

Boys as young as seven years old can begin studies at Tengboche Monastery. They learn Buddhist teachings, as well as reading, writing, history, and other subjects. By age twenty, they are ready to take their final vows as a monk. The monks' day begins early in the morning with group prayer. Study and meditation take up much of the rest of the day. Monks take turns with daily chores such as running the kitchen. Younger monks gather firewood, go shopping, and serve tea. Sometimes monks visit local homes to pray for someone who is sick or having difficulties. The monks' families and communities support them, considering it an honor to take part in the community's spiritual life.

MOUNTAINEERING: A CHANGE OF CULTURE

Sherpa life began to change in the 1920s when the British began climbing Mount Everest. On the very first British expedition in 1921, mountaineers discovered the remarkable physical traits of the Sherpas. With their climbing expertise and dedication, Sherpas were not only great porters, but ideal guides and life-saving team members. Ever since then, Sherpas have been an essential part of Everest climbing expeditions.

By the 1960s, hordes of climbers and trekkers were pouring into the Khumbu Valley. This had an enormous impact on traditional Sherpa culture. A farmer or yak herder could make much more money as a guide, porter, or cook on an Everest expedition. Ordinary householders could rent out rooms to trekkers. In time, the entire Sherpa economy came to depend on mountaineering.

"A good Sherpa can make maybe $2,000 in a season," says Ang Phurba, a Sherpa community leader. "Sirdars, or lead Sherpas, can make more, maybe $3,000." Some make as much as $7,000 a year. In contrast, the average per-person income in Nepal as a whole is about $260 a year. When adjusted for Nepal's lower cost of living, that equaled roughly $1,550 a year in 2005. With a much higher income from mountaineering, Sherpas are able to improve their lives. Many use the money to send their children to school. Others have opened businesses such as lodges, restaurants, or expedition companies.

Achievements and Tragedies

Gradually, Sherpas emerged from the role of helpers to highly respected mountaineers in their own right. Many Sherpas have set climbing records. Unfortunately, many of those who have died on Everest have been Sherpas, too. The most famous Sherpa mountaineer, of course, is Tenzing Norgay. His 1953 ascent with Edmund Hillary was the world's first climb to the summit. Tenzing's son Jamling Tenzing Norgay and his grandson Tashi Tenzing are mountaineers as well.

Tenzing Norgay: Tiger of the Snows

Tenzing Norgay (1914–1986) was born in Tsa-chu, in Tibet's Kharta Valley. His birth name was Namgyal Wangdi, but the lama at Rongbuk Monastery advised that his name be changed to Tenzing Norgay, meaning "wealthy follower of religion." Tenzing's father was a yak herder, but the family was reduced to poverty when disease killed their yaks. They then migrated to the village of Thame, Nepal. Although young Tenzing tended yaks, he dreamed of adventure. When he was a teenager, he moved to Darjeeling, India, to join mountaineering expeditions. After several rigorous climbs, he reached the level of sirdar, or lead guide, before his historic 1953 ascent of Mount Everest. Later, Tenzing operated the Himalayan Mountaineering Institute, a school for mountain-climbing guides in Darjeeling. His autobiography is titled *Tiger of the Snows*.

Pasang Lhamu Sherpa made history in 1993 when she became the first Nepali woman to climb Mount Everest. Her achievement had a tragic ending, though. On her descent, she fell into a crevasse and died. Pemba Doma Sherpa was the first Nepali woman to climb Everest's north side successfully. Sadly, she fell to her death in 2007 while climbing Lhotse.

As of 2008 Apa Sherpa had reached Everest's summit eighteen times, setting the record for number of successful summits. Ang Rita Sherpa, known as the Snow Leopard, began working as a porter when he was fifteen. By the time he retired in 1999, he had climbed Mount Everest ten times without using supplemental oxygen.

Babu Chhiri Sherpa made headlines in 1999 when he spent the longest-ever time on the summit of Everest. Fulfilling a personal dream, he pitched a tent on the top of the peak and slept there, staying twenty-one hours without supplemental oxygen. Having reached the summit ten times, he suffered a fatal fall into a crevasse in 2001. These are just a few of the achievements—and tragedies—of Sherpa mountaineers.

THE TIBET SIDE OF EVEREST

The Tibet side of Mount Everest is more lightly populated than the Nepal side. However, various groups of Tibetan peoples have made homes in the Kama, Kharta, Kangshung, Rongbuk, and other valleys. Like the Sherpas to the south, they have a traditional lifestyle of farming and seminomadic herding. Small, scattered settlements dot

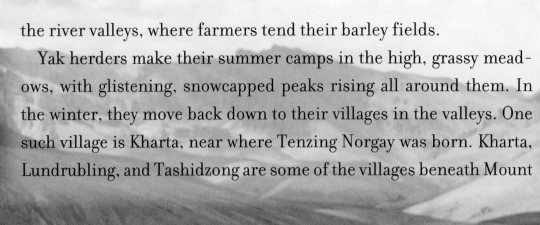

the river valleys, where farmers tend their barley fields.

Yak herders make their summer camps in the high, grassy mead-ows, with glistening, snowcapped peaks rising all around them. In the winter, they move back down to their villages in the valleys. One such village is Kharta, near where Tenzing Norgay was born. Kharta, Lundrubling, and Tashidzong are some of the villages beneath Mount

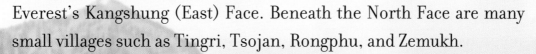

Everest's Kangshung (East) Face. Beneath the North Face are many small villages such as Tingri, Tsojan, Rongphu, and Zemukh.

Here, too, native people follow Tibetan Buddhism. It has not always been easy. During China's Cultural Revolution (1966–1976), religion was suppressed. Many beautiful monasteries were destroyed, their precious ornaments stolen, and their ancient writings burned.

Yak herders break for a meal on the Tibetan Plateau.

Today, the Chinese government tolerates a certain amount of religious practice. Regardless of political conditions, though, Buddhism is a basic element in Tibetan culture. Most Tibetans—especially those in remote communities such as the Everest region—kept their ancient faith alive.

Hidden Valleys, Sacred Caves

According to tradition, the great Buddhist master Padmasambhava hid *beyuls*, or sacred valleys, throughout the Himalayas. These valleys were to be refuges where people could hide in times of conflict and religious persecution. In the beyuls, they would enjoy peace, a bounteous environment, and spiritual freedom. This concept inspired the Western legend of Shangri-La.

Some say these valleys will remain hidden until they are needed. Others say that 108 valleys in the Himalayan region are beyuls, including the Khumbu and Khembalung valleys of Nepal and the Kama and Kharta valleys of Tibet.

Many holy sites are scattered throughout Tibet's hidden valleys. Near Pethang Ringmo is the sacred lake Tse Chu and a sacred cave where Padmasambhava is said to have meditated. Within the cave are prayer rooms where pilgrims pray and make offerings. A hidden cave near Rongbuk Monastery is one of the many other caves associated with Padmasambhava.

Rongbuk Monastery rises in the Rongbuk Valley near the foot of Rongbuk Glacier. At about 16,500 feet (5,000 m), it is the highest monastery on Earth. This was once a great Buddhist center, where people from as far away as Mongolia came for religious festivals. Established in either 1899 or 1902, it was destroyed during the Cultural Revolution. Now it is gradually being restored. The monastery is home to both monks and nuns, or women leading religious lives.

IMPACTS OF MOUNTAINEERING

The mountain-climbing craze impacts Tibet in different ways than it affects Nepal. Climbers often stop at Rongbuk Monastery to receive blessings. However, China has built the Rongbuk Hotel near the monastery. Another hotel is planned for the North Face Base Camp, which is served by a cellular phone tower.

The village outside Base Camp is full of merchants' tents, where people sell liquor, food, and climbing gear. This is one of the few ways local people can benefit from mountaineering. Since China took over Tibet in 1950, the government has controlled tourism. The Chinese tourism office collects fees from trekkers, and very little of the money goes to the local people and their communities. To boost Everest tourism, China has also expanded its road system to the region. Nomads along the routes have been forced to relocate to towns, where they have no way to make a living.

Mountaineering has had a more positive impact on the Sherpas of Nepal. In the 1950s, Sherpa communities had no schools, hospitals, electricity, or telephones. Now they have all these services, as well as satellite TV. Many young Sherpas abandon their traditional culture. They leave their villages and go to Kathmandu to get jobs on expeditions.

Still, in many ways, life on both sides of Mount Everest is the same as it has always been. Farmers still sow and harvest their crops, and herders still move their yaks as the seasons come and go. Buddhist devotion, along with Buddhist values of kindness and compassion, remain a part of everyday life.

A Sherpa shopkeeper keeps an eye out for tourists. ▶▶

SIX

A Mountain at Risk

From a distance, Mount Everest seems a crisp, clean expanse of natural landscape in perfect balance. A closer look tells a different story, though. Both human and natural forces endanger the Everest environment. Vegetation is stripped from the hillsides, soil washes into the streams, and floods sweep villages away. Waste litters the mountainsides all the way up to the summit. Local communities and international organizations are working to protect this precious wonder of nature.

STRIPPING THE HILLSIDES

Deforestation is one of the most serious environmental problems in the Everest region. At higher altitudes, local people have always gathered dwarf junipers, alpine cushion plants, and other shrubs for their household cooking and heating fires and for ceremonial fires at the monasteries. Through natural regrowth, the plant levels had remained stable. The lure of Mount Everest changed that balance, though.

◄ *Castoff supplies left by previous expeditions litter the slopes of Mount Everest.*

Tens of thousands of people visit the Everest region every year. Some are experienced mountaineers planning to climb the peak. Most, however, are amateur climbers or adventurous tourists. They come to enjoy the scenery, visit monasteries, or experience local culture. Many climb no higher than Base Camp.

With the yearly flood of visitors, people began harvesting vast quantities of juniper and other plants for campfires. At lower altitudes, forest trees were cut to build hundreds of lodges, teahouses, restaurants, and shops to serve visitors. These establishments kept consuming wood, using many times more firewood than an ordinary household needs.

Grasses came under increasing pressure, too. Herders have always grazed their yaks in the high alpine meadows. Once the climbing season begins, droves of yaks ascend the slopes carrying expedition equipment. These yaks need to eat, too, and they overgraze the herders' pastures.

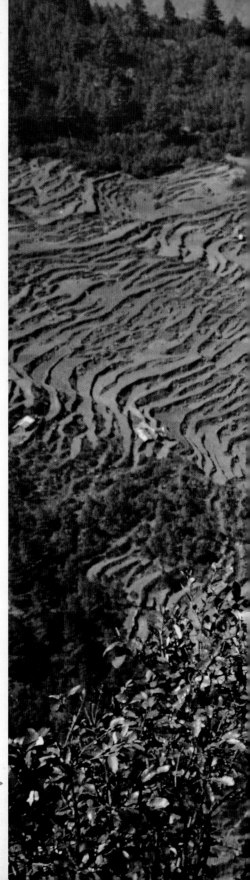

Hillsides have been depleted of ▶▶ forestland to make way for crops.

Soil erosion has been one effect of these activities. Trees, shrubs, and grasses on the hillsides hold the soil in place. As they are removed, the thin, fragile soils easily wash away in the monsoon rains. This, in turn, leads to water pollution. Loose soil washes into the rivers and streams, making the water unfit for drinking.

WILDLIFE ISSUES

Another effect of deforestation is the loss of wildlife habitats. Musk deer, Himalayan black bears, red pandas, snow leopards, and many bird species depend on thick vegetation. They take cover among the trees and bushes and find their food there. Deforestation forces them to seek food and shelter somewhere else. This endangers the region's **biodiversity**. Poaching, or illegal hunting, takes its toll on wildlife, too. Poachers have hunted the Himalayan musk deer until it has become an endangered species.

The Nepali government established Sagarmatha National Park in 1976. It covers the Everest region from Namche Bazar up to the top of the mountain. The park banned hunting, and armed guards began patrolling the park for poachers. Gradually, their work has paid off. Populations of musk deer and Himalayan tahr have been growing since the early 1990s. These animals are known as indicator species. That means their presence is a sign of environmental changes that affect many other species as well. There have been more sightings of the rare snow leopard in Sagarmatha, too.

CONSERVATION: A COMMUNITY EFFORT

Both local and international organizations are working to protect Mount Everest's landscape. Once Sagarmatha National Park was established, it set forth strict regulations for the use of forest trees and fuel wood. Cutting trees for construction was prohibited. So was the use of wood fuel by mountaineering groups. Climbers were required to use portable kerosene or gas stoves. In the 1980s, wood fuel was banned in teashops and lodges. Several mountainside villages now have kerosene depots where people can buy kerosene.

Many Sherpa families live in Sagarmatha National Park. They, too, have been encouraged to use kerosene, but this is an expensive fuel for them. To address the energy problem, several small hydroelectric projects have been built in mountainside villages. Using waterpower from rivers and streams, these projects bring electricity to homes and businesses. Now more and more people are setting aside their wood-burning stoves and using small cooking heaters. Many lodges and restaurants are also switching to electric hot plates, microwaves, mixers, rice cookers, refrigerators, and room heaters.

A family learns about environmentalism at Sagarmatha National Park.

Sir Edmund Hillary was the driving force behind the formation of Sagarmatha National Park. He was saddened to watch the region degrade over the years. In 1960 Hillary founded the Himalayan Trust. Through the trust, he opened schools, hospitals, and other facilities for local Sherpas. In 1982, to reduce the loss of vegetation, the trust purchased and removed about four hundred goats that had been grazing on the slopes. Eventually, goats were banned from the park altogether.

The Sagarmatha Community Agro-forestry Project (SCAFP) began in 1996. It is jointly managed by government agencies and the World Wildlife Fund (WWF). The project introduces local people to agro-forestry projects such as plant nurseries. People raise trees on small plantations and replant young trees on the hillsides to reestablish forests there. The project also teaches people **sustainable** ways to use forest resources.

Guardians of the Forest

The Sherpa people have a traditional system of forest management called *shinga nawa*, or *shingo ngawa*. The *nawas* were guardians of the forest. They allocated forest resources and made sure people kept local rules for forest use. *Nawas* regulated grazing, tree harvesting, and other activities. The *shinga nawa* system has been reinstated in Sagarmatha National Park. *Nawas* now patrol the forests to prevent illegal cutting, protect tree plantations, and report wildlife poaching.

LITTERING, GARBAGE, AND WASTES

When the first humans set foot on Mount Everest in 1921, it was a pristine environmental paradise. Sadly, after decades of camping and climbing activities, the mountainsides began to look like a junkyard. Discarded equipment such as tents, ropes, and empty oxygen cylinders—and even a crashed helicopter—littered the mountainsides. Water bottles, aluminum cans, plastic bags, toilet paper, and human waste were scattered up and down the slopes. Everest began to be called the "world's highest garbage dump."

The filth on Mount Everest became an international disgrace. It alarmed Sherpa residents, local environmental organizations, and the world community. Environmentalists point out that plastic can take 220 years to decompose. Toilet paper may be **biodegradable**, but at 13,000 feet (4,000 m), it can take thirty years to decompose. That is a much lower altitude than Everest Base Camp. At Mount Everest's highest elevations, nothing decomposes.

To deal with the pollution problem, the Sagarmatha Pollution Control Committee (SPCC) was formed in 1991. Headed by

A Japanese mountaineer shows a sampling of the more than 5,000 pounds of trash he collected on Mount Everest.

the abbot of Tengboche Monastery, the committee was funded by the WWF and the Himalayan Trust. The cleanup began with about eighty local volunteers. They hauled five hundred yak loads of garbage—about 33 tons—from the lower slopes of Mount Everest. By 2003 SPCC had collected more than 2,000 tons of garbage. Other countries have joined in the cleanup, too.

Human waste presents a special problem. It freezes during the winter, making it hard to remove. When the snows begin to melt in the spring, it thaws, releasing an odor, and pollutes the waterways. In 2008 a Sherpa trekking agency conducted a mission called Eco Everest Expedition 2008. It targeted human waste, from Base Camp to the summit. Team members carried biodegradable bags in which waste material decomposes. Park rules for human waste disposal now require the use of portable plastic drums and deeply dug pits.

MELTING GLACIERS AND CLIMATE CHANGE

Mount Everest's glaciers are retreating. That is, the ice is melting much faster than each year's new snow and ice can replace. According to Jamling Tenzing Norgay, "The glacier on which Base Camp sits has melted to such a degree that it is now at a lower altitude." Base camp now sits 130 feet (40 m) lower than in did when Jamling's father first climbed the peak in 1953.

Ordinarily, a glacier undergoes some melting in the spring and summer. Then it builds up more snow and ice in the fall and winter, maintaining its size. Everest's glaciers, however, are shrinking.

A Waste Management System

The Sagarmatha Pollution Control Committee has established a waste management system for all Everest expedition teams. When climbers enter Sagarmatha National Park, they must pay an environmental deposit of four thousand dollars. They receive bags for burnable, recyclable, and nonrecyclable wastes. When the teams come back down, they present their sorted wastes for inspection. Only after meeting all the regulations do they get their deposit back.

Many scientists believe that this is due to global warming. As factories and vehicles emit carbon dioxide and other gases into the atmosphere, the gases trap heat close to the earth, warming the entire planet. Some scientists insist that global warming is a natural cycle of the earth's climate. Regardless of the causes, researchers say global warming is drastically changing the appearance, ecology, and climate of Mount Everest.

Glacier retreat has a devastating impact on the landscape and on human lives. The meltwater fills rivers and swells glacial lakes. When the lakes fill up with too much water, they can burst their banks, causing massive floods in the valleys downstream. This is called a glacial lake outburst flood, or GLOF. These floods kill people and animals and destroy forests, farms, and buildings.

In 1985 the Dig Tsho glacial lake in the Khumbu region overflowed, sending a torrent of water rushing downhill. It destroyed fourteen bridges, a hydroelectric plant, and most of a village, along with its cultivated fields. Many other glacial lakes in the region have also burst.

Scientists are now identifying glacial lakes that may be at risk. Using satellite imagery, they are mapping and monitoring the lakes. An international team of scientists joined the Eco Everest Expedition 2008. After inspecting the Dig Tsho site, they made extensive studies of Mount Everest's glacial lakes. They plan to develop early warning systems for floods and to help communities adapt to the dangers.

The Eco Everest scientists hope to draw attention to the dangers of global warming. They point out that industrialized countries are causing most of the climate change. However, the effects are harming people in underdeveloped areas. Himalayan glaciers not only present a flood danger when they melt; they also provide the water supply for more than 1 billion people who live downstream. This is a grave, worldwide concern, according to Dr. Andreas Schild, director of the International Centre for Integrated Mountain Development. "The changes taking place currently are alarming," he says, "and the time to act is now."

Meltwater from retreating glaciers ▶▶
threatens the landscape and people
who live near Mount Everest.

Like all things on Earth, Mount Everest is subject to change. It has survived among the Himalayan peaks for millions of years—growing, shifting, and changing its contours with the passage of time. Over the years, people have approached the mountain as a deity, a natural wonder, a source of livelihood, and the ultimate mountaineering challenge. Unfortunately, human activities have altered Everest's landscape far beyond the natural course of events. To reverse this pattern, we need to embrace our role as caretakers of Earth. Thus we can preserve the grandeur of Mount Everest for generations to come.

Glossary

avalanche sudden, rapid flows of snow down a mountainside

biodegradable made of substances that break down quickly through the action of bacteria

biodiversity the number and variety of plants and animals within a region

deforestation the removal or destruction of forest trees

monsoon seasonal winds blowing from the Indian Ocean toward Asia, bringing heavy precipitation

mountaineers people who pursue mountain climbing as a serious sport

reincarnation the belief that, after death, a being's soul is reborn in a new body

Sherpas people of a Tibetan ethnic group living in the Everest region; expert Himalayan mountaineers, porters, and guides

surveying taking measurements to determine the exact locations of points on the earth and distances between them in order to make geographical maps

sustainable a way of using natural resources without destroying them for future use

Fast Facts

Name: Mount Everest

Nepali name: Sagarmatha ("Goddess of the Sky")

Tibetan name: Chomolungma or Qomolangma ("Goddess Mother of the World")

Distinction: Highest peak on Earth

Height: 29,035 feet (8,850 m) above sea level

Himalaya Mountains

Mountain range: Himalaya Mountains

Location: Nepal and the Tibet Autonomous Region of China

Named after: Sir George Everest, British surveyor-general of India (1830–1843)

Identified as highest: 1852, by Radhanath Sikdar

First climbing expedition: 1921, by a British team including George Mallory

First summit climb: 1953, by Edmund Hillary and Tenzing Norgay

Major glaciers: Khumbu Glacier (Nepal); Rongbuk Glacier, Kangshung Glacier (Tibet)

Average temperature:

    Summit, January: −33° Fahrenheit (−36 °C)

    Summit, July: −2° Fahrenheit (−19 °C)

Average precipitation:

    Namche Bazar: 39 inches (99 cm)

    Tengboche: 41 inches (104 cm)

Major villages: Namche Bazar, Khumjung, Tengboche, Pangboche, Dingboche, Pheriche, Thame (Nepal); Kharta, Lundrubling, Tashidzong, Rongphu, Tingri, Tsojan, Zemukh (Tibet)

Ethnic groups: Sherpas (Nepal); Tibetans (Tibet)

Animals: Himalayan tahrs, langurs, jackals, Himalayan black bears, red pandas, snow leopards, Himalayan musk deers, gorals, serows, Impeyan pheasants, blood pheasants, choughs, snow pigeons, snowcocks

Plants: Rhododendrons, junipers, silver firs, hemlocks, blue pines, alpine grasses, alpine cushion plants

Cultural landmarks: Tengboche, Pangboche, Thame, and Khumjung monasteries (Nepal); Rongbuk Monastery (Tibet)

Himalayan black bear

Protected areas: Sagarmatha National Park (Nepal); Qomolangma Nature Reserve (Tibet)

Natural resources: Forests, grasslands, and water for irrigation, household use, and hydroelectric power

Economic activities: Tourism, yak and cattle herding, farming, trade

Greatest threats: Deforestation, soil erosion, water pollution, human littering

Find Out More

BOOKS

Chester, Jonathan. *The Young Adventurer's Guide To Everest: From Avalanche to Zopkio*. Berkeley, CA: Tricycle Press, 2005.

Dowswell, Paul. *True Everest Adventures*. London: Usborne, 2004.

Kodas, Michael. *High Crimes: The Fate of Everest in an Age of Greed*. New York: Hyperion, 2008.

Lappi, Megan. *Mount Everest: The Highest Mountain in the World*. New York: Weigl Publishers, 2006.

O'Shei, Tim. *Left for Dead!: Lincoln Hall's Story of Survival*. Mankato, MN: Capstone Press, 2007.

Whipple, Heather. *Hillary & Norgay: To the Top of Mount Everest*. New York: Crabtree, 2007.

DVDs

Everest: Beyond the Limit; The Complete 1st Season (3 discs). Discovery Channel, 2007.

Everest: Beyond the Limit; The Complete 2nd Season (4 discs). Discovery Channel, 2008.

Sherpa: The Proving Grounds. CustomFlix, 2006.

Team Everest: A Himalayan Journey. Danger Dog Films, 2008.

Touching the Void. MGM, 2004.

Destination: Himalayas—Where Earth Meets Sky

http://library.thinkquest.org/10131/javascriptmenu_final.html

Explores the geography, geological history, wildlife, and environmental problems of the Himalayan region.

Everest: Measure of a Mountain

www.nationalgeographic.com/features/99/everest/index2.html

National Geographic's examination of Mount Everest's geology and history, along with day-by-day reports from an expedition team.

NOVA Online: Everest

www.pbs.org/wgbh/nova/everest/

An in-depth look at Mount Everest's geography, cultures, historic expeditions, and popular climbing routes, as well as the human body's functions at high altitudes.

Sagarmatha National Park

www.south-asia.com/dnpwc/Sagarmatha%20national%20Park/sagindex.html

Nepal's site on the climate, plants, animals, glaciers, Sherpas, and trekking routes in Sagarmatha National Park.

Index

Page numbers in **boldface** are illustrations and charts.

ABOUT THE AUTHOR

Ann Heinrichs of Chicago is the author of more than two hundred books for children and young adults. Their topics range from U.S. and world history, geography, and cultures to science, nature, and grammar. For Marshall Cavendish Benchmark, she has written Nature's Wonders *The Nile, The Sahara,* and *The Amazon Rain Forest.* An avid world traveler, Ann has toured parts of Europe, Asia, Africa, and the Middle East, as well as most of the United States. She has climbed Mount Sinai in Egypt, the Sangre de Cristo Mountains in New Mexico, and the Sierra Nevada on the California-Nevada border, but she will probably never climb Mount Everest.